Contents

Gastric sleeve surgery

Gastric Sleeve Recipes: Discover how to make fast and easy recipes after your surgery. A step by step guide to Maximize Your Weight Loss Results. Learn how to cook more than 50+ recipes.

Alex Martinez

Introduction

Gastric sleeve surgery--also called sleeve gastrectomy--is a kind of bariatric (weight loss) surgery. Gastric sleeve surgery involves reducing the size of your tummy so that you feel full after eating just a little bit of food. Although this surgery is an effective way of losing weight, it is not a permanent alternative. Patients should be willing and ready to commit to lifelong healthier eating and exercise habits to maintain weight loss and prevent complications.

As stated by the American Society for Metabolic and Bariatric Surgery, gastric sleeve surgery is the most commonly performed bariatric procedure in the United States. Gastric sleeve surgery is an inpatient procedure conducted with a bariatric surgeon at a hospital or surgical center under general anesthesia. This scheduled, one- to - surgery might be carried out in adults in addition to teens.2

With gastric sleeve surgery, the physician removes about 80 percent of the gut so as to make a bigger stomach. The new gut is tubular in shape and about the size of a banana.3 With this decrease, patients feel full for many hours after eating only a tiny quantity of food--consequently, reducing their total consumption.

Apart from making a bigger stomach, gastric sleeve surgery eliminates the gut cells that normally create the hunger hormone ghrelin. This reduction in hormone production means patients often experience a decrease in appetite, which could further result in weight reduction.

Different Surgical Approaches

The gastric sleeve process is usually done laparoscopically, using minimally invasive methods.4Less commonly, the surgery is available, meaning that the surgeon makes a large incision in the patient's stomach to get the gut.

In comparison to gastric bypass surgery, yet another popular weight reduction process, gastric sleeve surgery is related to lower risks and is technically easier to do.5 Gastric sleeve surgery is also not regarded as extreme by sufferers, since it's simply a restrictive process and doesn't entail reducing nutrient absorption from the tiny intestines.

Chapter 1 what is gastric sleeve?

Shed Weight and Stay better Using the Vertical Sleeve

Vertical sleeve gastrectomy: A milder approach to weight reduction surgery

Bariatric surgery could be lifesaving for individuals that Fight with obesity. A relatively new alternative is that the perpendicular sleeve gastrectomy, a minimally-invasive surgery that shrinks the stomach and decreases the body's "hunger hormone".

Restricting stomach size and food ingestion

Throughout the process, 75 percent of the gut is removed, leaving the residual portion shaped like a narrow tube or sleeve. The stomach usually stretches whenever someone eats, and to curb overeating, so which portion of the gut is removed through a vertical sleeve gastrectomy.

"We leave the individual with a very narrow stomach that is Inelastic," states Kevin McGill, M.D., a typical and bariatric surgeon in Piedmont.

Reducing the "hunger hormone"

Another advantage to patients is that the vertical sleeve Gastrectomy eliminates the section of the stomach that creates ghrelin, the appetite hormone.

"Nownot only does one not consume a Whole Lot, but your mind is okay with this," clarifies Dr. McGill. "You do not have the exact same satiety variables floating about."

Gastric bypass versus vertical sleeve gastrectomy

"What we like about this surgery is it is not quite as [complicated] as a gastric bypass," he states.

Both vertical sleeve gastrectomy and gastric bypass Procedures decrease the size of their stomach and restrict food consumption, but gastric bypass surgery also eliminates elements of their intestines. This decreases the calories and nutrients the body absorbs, but it could also result in malnutrition in certain patients.

Cosmetic surgery versus laparoscopic weight loss surgery

The robotic version of the surgery is similar to this Laparoscopic method, states Dr. McGill, however, the autonomous tool permits surgeons to view three-dimensionally and possess an increased range of hand movement in addition to increased depth understanding.

Piedmont: Advisors in weight loss surgery

"In Piedmont, we have been very privileged to be about the Top edge of bariatric surgery," he states. "We were among those very first couple of institutions in the country to present the sleeve gastrectomy and we had been among those first couple to begin performing robotic surgery for bariatrics."

Piedmont bariatric surgeons work closely with patients during their weight loss travels, from pre-surgery appointments to postoperative care.

What exactly does gastric sleeve surgery demand?

1 approach to tackle obesity would be with regular surgery. This Kind of surgery involves removing or diminishing the size of

your tummy. Bariatric surgery typically contributes to rapid weight reduction.

Gastric sleeve surgery is one of several Kinds of bariatric Surgery choices. Medical professionals typically call it vertical sleeve gastrectomy.

In this Guide, you'll have a closer look at what is involved in gastric sleeve surgery, such as its efficacy and potential complications.

Unless there are complications, you should have the Ability to go Home within two or three days following the surgery.

Is it successful?

Gastric sleeve surgery helps you Drop weight in two manners:

- Your Stomach is considerably smaller in order to feel full and stop eating earlier. As a result, that you take in fewer calories.

- The component of the stomach that generates ghrelin -- a hormone that is connected with appetite -- has been eliminated, which means you are much less hungry.

According to the American Society of Metabolic and Allergic Surgery, you can expect to lose at least 50 per cent of your extra weight over the 18 to 24 weeks after gastric sleeve surgery. Some people today lose 60 to 70 percent Trusted Source.

It is Important to Keep in Mind that this Is Only Going to happen if you Are dedicated to adhering to the diet and exercise program recommended by your physician. By embracing these lifestyle modifications, you are more inclined to keep the weight off long term.

Weight reduction benefits

Losing a significant Number of excess weights can improve Your wellbeing also make it less difficult to carry out many daily tasks.

Another important advantage of weight reduction is that the reduced risk Of obesity-related wellness conditions. These include:

- Type 2 diabetes

- Significant cholesterol (hyperlipidemia)

• Significant Blood pressure (hypertension)

• Obstructive Sleep apnea

Who's a fantastic candidate for this surgery?

Bariatric surgery of any type, such as gastric sleeve Surgery, is just considered a choice when powerful attempts to boost your diet and exercise habits, and also the usage of weight-loss drugs, have not worked.

Even after that, you have to meet specific standards to be eligible for A regular procedure. These standards are based on the own body mass index (BMI) and if you have some obesity-related wellness conditions.

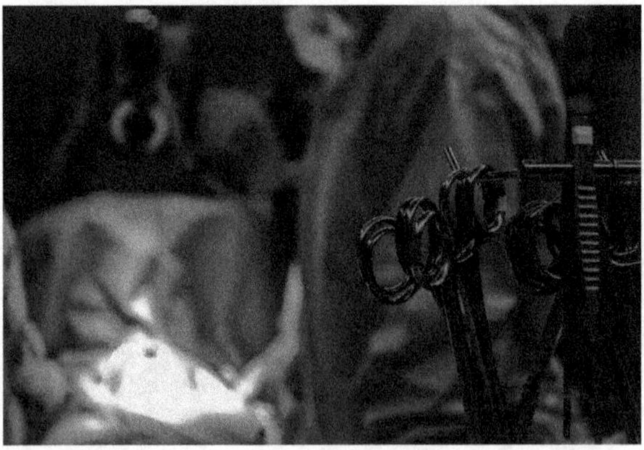

Qualifying conditions:

• Intense (morbid) obesity (BMI score of 40 or greater)

• Obesity (BMI score of 35 to 39) with one important obesity-related condition

Sometimes, gastric sleeve surgery is completed if you are Obese but do not fulfill the standards for obesity, however, you get a substantial health condition associated with your weight.

What are the complications and risks?

Gastric sleeve surgery is known as a relatively safe procedure. But like all significant surgeries, there may be dangers and complications.

Some complications may happen after any surgery. All these include:

• Hemorrhage. Bleeding in the wound or within your body may result in shock when it is severe.

• Deep vein thrombosis (DVT). Surgery as well as the healing process can boost your chance of a blood clot forming on your vein, usually in a leg vein.

• Pulmonary embolism. A pulmonary embolism can occur when a part of a blood clot breaks off and travels to your lungs.

• Irregular heartbeat. Surgery may boost the danger of an irregular pulse, particularly atrial fibrillation.

• Pneumonia. Pain can permit you to take shallow breaths that may result in a lung disease, such as pneumonia.

Gastric sleeve surgery may have added complications. A few possible side effects that are specific to this surgery include:

• Gastric leaks. Stomach fluids can flow in the suture line on your gut where it had been stitched back together.

• Stenosis. Section of your gastric sleeve may shut, resulting in an obstruction in your stomach.

• Vitamin deficiencies. The part of your gut that is eliminated is partially responsible for the absorption of vitamins that your body needs. If you don't take vitamin supplements, then this may result in deficiencies.

• Heartburn (GERD). Reshaping your gut can cause or aggravate heartburn. This may normally be treated with over-the-counter drugs.

It is Important to Keep in Mind that changing your diet and Exercise habits are crucial to losing the weight and keeping it off following gastric sleeve surgery. It is potential to gain the weight back if you

• eat also much

• consume an unhealthy diet

• exercise too little

Other concerns

Another Frequent concern, especially Once You Eliminate Lots of Weight fast, is that the massive number of surplus skin you might be left with as the pounds drop away. This is a frequent complication of gastric sleeve surgery.

This excess skin could be removed if it disturbs you. But bear in mind it may take around 18 months for the body to stabilize following gastric sleeve surgery. That is why it's generally better to wait until considering a skin removal process. Until then, you might want to try out some strategies for tightening loose skin.

Another thing to think about before choosing to have gastric Sleeve surgery is that, unlike any other regular surgeries, gastric sleeve surgery is permanent. If you aren't satisfied with the outcome, your tummy cannot be transformed back to how it was.

How can your diet alter following gastric sleeve surgery?

Before gastric sleeve surgery is completed, you typically must consent to particular lifestyle modifications recommended by your physician. These changes are supposed to assist you reach and maintain weight loss.

One of these changes involves eating a healthy diet for the remainder of your life.

Your physician will recommend the very best gastric sleeve diet to get you after your surgery. The dietary modifications your surgeon proposes may be like the overall dietary guidelines under.

Dietary changes

- Two weeks Prior surgery. Boost protein, lower carbs, and remove sugar from the dietplan.

- Two days before and the first week following surgery. Ingest only clear fluids which are caffeine- and - carbonation-free.

- For the Next three months. It's possible to add pureed food into your dietplan.

You will usually have the Ability to eat regular, Healthful food about 1 month following your surgery. You might discover that you just eat less than prior to the process since you will get full fast and will not feel overly hungry.

Your restricted diet and smaller foods may cause some Nutritional deficiencies. It is important to compensate for this by choosing multivitamins, calcium supplements, a monthly B-12 shot, and many others as recommended by your physician.

Is it covered by insurance?

In the USA, most health insurers realize that obesity is a risk factor for other health conditions that may cause serious medical issues. Because of this, many insurance businesses cover gastric sleeve surgery when you've got a qualifying state.

In accordance with the Centers of Medicare & Medicare Services (CMS), Medicare will cover gastric sleeve surgery if you meet the following requirements:

- Your BMI is 35 or greater

- You've one or more obesity-related health ailments

• You had been not able to eliminate the weight by simply modifying your diet and exercise habits or simply by taking drugs

Medicare does not cover gastric sleeve surgery in case you are Obese but do not possess an obesity-related health state.

Without health insurance policy, the price of gastric Sleeve surgery may vary widely from 1 area into another, and also from 1 centre to another in the exact same geographical location. Normally, the price could range from $15,000 to over $25,000.

Given this wide variation, it is Ideal to study and Speak to Several operative and surgeons facilities to find one you are familiar with -- and also one which satisfies your budget.

Gastric sleeve surgery is one of several Kinds of bariatric Surgery choices. It works by making your stomach smaller so that you eat less. Since the size of the gut is reduced, you will also realize that you are less hungry.

To be eligible for gastric sleeve surgery, you need to meet specific criteria. You have to show that you have attempted other weight-loss strategies -- such as diet, exercise, and weight loss drugs -- with no success. Other qualifying standards comprise your BMI and if you have some obesity-related wellness conditions.

Should you follow a healthy diet and exercise regimen frequently after gastric sleeve surgery, you could have the ability to shed more than 50 per cent of your extra weight over 24 months.

However, as with the Majority of surgical procedures, there's the danger of side effects and complications. If you are considering gastric sleeve surgery, speak to your physician about whether you are eligible for this process and if it is a secure solution for you.

Summary

Sleeve gastrectomy, also called a vertical sleeve Gastrectomy, is a surgical weight reduction process. This process is normally done laparoscopically, which involves integrating small instruments through multiple tiny incisions in the upper gut. Throughout sleeve gastrectomy, about 80 percent of the gut is removed, leaving a tube-shaped gut about the size and shape of a banana.

Limiting the size of your tummy limits the amount of Food you can eat. Additionally, the process prompts hormonal fluctuations that help with weight reduction. These exact same hormonal changes also help alleviate conditions related to being overweight, such as hypertension or cardiovascular disease.

Why it is done

Sleeve gastrectomy is done to Assist You shed weight And lower your risk of possibly life-threatening weight-related health difficulties, such as:

- Heart Disorder
- High Blood pressure
- High Cholesterol
- Obstructive Sleep apnea
- Type 2 diabetes
- Stroke

- Cancer

- Infertility

Sleeve gastrectomy is normally performed just after you have attempted To get rid of weight by boosting your diet and workout habits.

Generally, sleeve gastrectomy surgery may be an option for you if:

- Your Entire Body Mass index (BMI) is 40 or greater (extreme obesity).

- Your BMI Is 35 to 39.9 (obesity), and you also get a severe weight-related health issue, like type 2 diabetes, higher blood pressure or severe sleep apnea. Sometimes, you might be eligible for certain kinds of weight loss surgery if your BMI is 30 to 34 and you've got severe weight-related health issues.

You must also be willing to create permanent changes to direct a healthier lifestyle. You could have to take part in long-term follow-up programs which have tracking your nourishment, your way of life and behaviour, along with your medical problems.

Check with your Medical Insurance program or your regional Medicare or Medicaid office to discover if your policy insures weight loss surgery.

Hazards

Just like any significant surgery, sleeve gastrectomy poses possible health dangers, both at the brief term and long term.

Risks Connected with sleeve gastrectomy can comprise:

- Excessive Infection

- Infection

- Adverse Responses to anesthesia

- Blood Infection

• Lung or breathing problems

• Leaks In the cut edge of the gut

Longer term dangers and complications of sleeve gastrectomy surgery can include:

• Gastrointestinal Obstruction

• Hernias

• Gastroesophageal reflux

• Low blood sugar (hypoglycemia)

• Malnutrition

• Vomiting

Quite rarely, complications of sleeve gastrectomy could be fatal.

The best way to prepare

In the weeks leading up to a surgery, You Might Be required to begin a physical activity program and also to stop any tobacco usage.

Right before your process, You Might Have limitations on Drinking and eating and which drugs you may take.

Now's a Fantastic time to plan ahead to your restoration after surgery. For example, arrange for assistance at home when you feel you'll want it.

What you could expect

Sleeve gastrectomy is performed from the hospital. Based on Your recovery, your hospital stay may last one or two nights.

Throughout the Process

The particulars of your surgery depend on your individual Situation along with the hospital or physician's practices. Some sleeve gastrectomies are complete with conventional big (open) incisions in the stomach. But sleeve gastrectomy is normally done laparoscopically, which involves integrating small instruments through multiple tiny incisions in the upper stomach.

You're given general anesthesia prior to your surgery starts. Anesthesia is medication that keeps you asleep and comfortable during surgery.

To execute a sleeve gastrectomy, the surgeon creates a Lean sleeve by stapling the stomach vertically and eliminating the bigger, curved region of the gut.

Surgery usually takes one or two hours. Following surgery, you awaken at a recovery room, where medical staff monitors you for some complications.

Following the process

Once sleeve gastrectomy, your diet starts with sugar-free, noncarbonated liquids to the first seven days, then progresses to pureed foods for 3 weeks and to regular foods about four weeks following your surgery. You'll be asked to take a multivitamin twice every day, a calcium supplement once daily, and a vitamin B-12 shot once a month .

You'll have regular medical evaluations to monitor Your Wellbeing In the first few months after weight loss surgery. You Might Need lab Testing, bloodwork and assorted exams.

You will experience changes since the body reacts to the rapid Weight reduction from the first three to six months following sleeve gastrectomy, such as:

- Body aches

- Feeling Tired, as though you've got the flu

- Feeling Chilly

- Dry skin

• Hair Thinning and baldness

• Disposition changes

Outcomes

Sleeve gastrectomy might offer long-term weight reduction. The Amount of weight you lose is dependent upon your shift in lifestyle customs. It's likely to shed approximately 60 percent, or more, of the excess weight over two decades.

Along with weight reduction, sleeve gastrectomy may enhance or solve conditions associated with being overweight, such as:

• Heart Disorder

• High Blood pressure

• High Cholesterol

• Obstructive Sleep apnea

• Type 2 diabetes

• Stroke

• Infertility

Sleeve gastrectomy surgery may also improve your ability to perform regular daily tasks, and will help improve your wellbeing.

When weight surgery does not work

It is likely not to shed sufficient weight or to regain weight after weight-loss surgery. This weight reduction can occur if you do not stick to the suggested lifestyle changes. If you often bite fatty foods, for example, you might have insufficient weight reduction. To assist prevent regaining weight, you have to make permanent healthful changes in your diet and get regular physical exercise and activity.

It is important to keep all your scheduled follow-up Appointments following weight-loss surgery so that your physician can track your progress. If you observe that you are not losing fat or you develop complications following your surgery, visit your physician immediately.

Chapter 2 Gastric Sleeve Diet

If you are intending on having gastric sleeve surgery, you are likely anticipating your body, and learning how to eat in a completely new way. Preparing for your own life after gastric sleeve surgery will probably be exciting, but hard, too.

The diet you'll be required to follow both before and following Surgery is quite specific and targeted toward helping recovery and preventing complications. As time advances, your diet will probably change toward assisting you to acquire wholesome eating habits, which means that you may continue to shed weight and, finally, keep a healthy weight for life.

Pre-gastric sleeve diet

A primary, presurgery dietary aim is decreasing your liver. If You are heavy, your liver probably has an accumulation of fat cells in and about it. That makes it bigger than it ought to be. Your liver is situated directly beside your gut. A too-large liver creates gastric sleeve surgery tougher for the doctor to perform, and more dangerous that you have done.

To prepare for the process, you'll be given a certain Diet to follow, starting two weeks prior to your scheduled surgery date. It is a rigorous diet that reduces calories in addition to carbohydrates, like candies, potatoes, and pasta. You may eat mostly lean protein, vegetables, and non - or no-calorie fluids. Your physician may provide you a caloric objective to stick to every day.

Two days before surgery, you may switch to a definite, Liquid diet. This may contain one no-sugar protein shake every day, as well as broth, water, decaffeinated tea or coffee, Jell-O, and sugar-free popsicles. Caffeinated and carbonated drinks should be avoided.

Week 1 diet

For the first week following the procedure, you'll continue with The exact same clear liquid diet that you followed closely in the days leading up to surgery. This helps to prevent postoperative complications, such as bowel obstruction, gastrointestinal migraines, nausea, constipation, and dehydration. Your body needs time to cure, and this routine can assist with that objective. Ideas to remember include:

- Make sure to drink lots of fluids. In case you have issues staying hydrated, speak with your physician about electrolyte drinks to test, for example low-calorie Gatorade.

- Do not drink anything with sugar. Sugar can lead to dumping syndrome, a complication due to an excessive amount of sugar entering the small intestine fast. This leads to severe nausea, nausea, fatigue, and even nausea. Sugar can also be high in empty calories. It needs to be prevented today and diminished in the long run.

• Caffeine can give rise to acid reflux and reflux, and should likewise be avoided.

• Carbonated Drinks, such as those with glucose, no-calorie possibilities, and seltzer, can contribute to bloating and gas. These should be avoided postoperatively and even long term.

Week Two diet

During the next week following surgery, you'll graduate into a full-liquid diet. Alternatives include:

• No-sugar Nutrition shakes, for example Ensure Light

• Instant Breakfast beverages

• shakes Created with protein powder

• Thin Broth and cream-based soups without balls -- tender soup noodles are fine in rather tiny quantities

- Unsweetened milk

- Sugar-free, nonfat pudding

- Sugar-free, nonfat frozen yogurt, ice cream, and sorbet

- Nonfat Plain Greek yogurt

- Fruit Juices without a preservative, diluted with water

- Thinned, Hot cereal, like Cream of Wheat, or oatmeal

In this age, you might feel that your desire increase. That's totally normal, but not a reason to consume good food. Your system remains not able to take care of solids. Vomiting and other complications may result. Filling up on fluids and preventing fat and sugar can help prepare one for the next phase of your dietplan. Carbonated beverages and caffeine should nevertheless be avoided.

Week 3 diet

During week three, you can add soft, pureed foods into your diet. Be certain that you eat slowly and chew food completely -- at least 25 occasions, if at all possible. Any low carb, sugar-free food which you may puree, such as lean protein sources and nonfibrous veggies, are okay. It is important to begin increasing your protein intake. If you do not enjoy the flavor of unsalted lean protein sources, continue to consume no-sugar protein shakes or even consume eggs every day. Foods to eat contain:

- jarred Infant food
- Silken tofu
- Cooked, pureed white fish
- Soft-scrambled or soft-boiled eggs
- Soup
- Cabin cheese
- canned Fruit

• mashed Bananas or quite ripe mango

• Hummus

• Pureed or mashed avocado

• Plain Greek yogurt

Continue to prevent chunked and strong foods, along with Caffeine, in this moment. It's also advisable to adhere with bland food with moderate or no seasoning. Spices may result in heartburn.

Week 4 diet

Now that you are one month post-surgery, you can Begin incorporating Solid foods into your diet. This is the opportunity to set your brand new healthy-eating abilities into action, complete force. Sugar and fat, such as high-fat milk, should nevertheless be avoided, as if hard-to-digest foods like beef, fibrous veggies, and nuts. Other foods to avoid include pasta, white potatoes, along with other high-carb choices. Caffeinated beverages can ordinarily be reintroduced, in moderation, in this moment. Foods you can add to your list include:

- Well-cooked Fish and poultry

- Well-cooked vegetables

- Candy potatoes

- Low-fat cheese

- Fruit

- Low-sugar Cereal

Week 5 diet and past

Now Which You Can eats solid food securely, it is time to place Your own new-normal eating strategy to long-term impact. Maintain the emphasis on lean protein and veggies, introducing one food at one time so you can track your own body's reaction. Foods you ought to avoid completely, or just eat occasion from that point forward, add sugary soda and sweets. The rest of the foods can be integrated back in till they activate symptoms.

Choose your foods wisely, choosing nutrient-dense Possibilities, and avoid empty calories. Eating three small meals every day, with snacks that are minimal, might help you follow your strategy. Also be certain you always stay hydrated.

Guidelines and Ideas

Post-surgical retrieval tips that can help you stay on track include:

• Utilize a Blender or food processor to puree foods.

• Learn to recognize the distinction between desire (bodily) and desire (mental/emotional).

• Do not overeat -- your tummy will extend punctually and stabilize in size.

• Chew gradually, and eat slowly.

• Prevent non-nutrient calories.

• Prevent concentrated sugars.

- Prevent Tran's fats and fried, processed, and fast foods.

- Prevent Dehydration by sipping water or low-fat variations of Gatorade.

- Do not consume and drink at precisely the exact same moment.

- Talk to Your physician about bariatric vitamins and nutritional supplements to choose exactly what you ought to take, and if.

- Construct Movement in your life. Begin with walking, and research different exercises that you like, like swimming, dance, and yoga.

- Prevent alcohol. Gastric sleeve surgery and other forms of bariatric surgeries can increase, and accelerate, alcohol effects.

- Prevent Nonsteroidal anti inflammatory medications (NSAIDs), such as Ibuprofen, aspirin, and naproxen. These kinds of over-the-counter pain medicines may diminish your tummy's natural, protective coating.

GASTRIC SLEEVE DIET: PRE-OP AND POST-OP GUIDELINES

Gastric sleeve surgery is a safe and clinically proven Method for reducing body fat loss. The process entails decreasing belly size by dividing the upper area of the gut, known as the fundus, by the remainder of the organ. A smaller tummy usually means a smaller appetite. You get full faster and are less inclined to overeat.

The Efficacy of gastric sleeve surgery is determined by a great Deal in your own pre-op and post-op diet. Following are a few tips on maximizing the profits from a top weight-loss process.

What's a Gastric Sleeve?

The gastric sleeve would be the practical part of the gut after gastric sleeve surgery, also known as a gastrectomy. It represents about 15 percent of their gut's unique quantity. The sleeve is separated by the remainder of the manhood, which plays no additional part in the human body's digestive process. Its modest size reduces hunger and assists in long-term weight management. Gastric sleeve surgery is irreversible -- it can't be reversed.

What Can I Eat Before Gastric Sleeve Surgery?

The pre-op diet plan is the food-consumption strategy for the period Leading up to a gastric sleeve process. Your diet is critical to the surgery's success for three reasons:

• It makes the process safer and simpler. The pre-op diet aids reduce fatty deposits around the liver, which enhances surgical accessibility into the gut.

• It enhances the danger of complications. Obesity raises the risk of health complications during and after surgery; weight reduction can counteract this threat.

• It begins you about the customs you will want to create a lifelong dedication to weight management. You will get the confidence which accompanies settings goals and attaining them.

Oftentimes, you ought to begin your pre-op diet to get a Gastric sleeve surgery three months before your procedure. Please speak with your program dietician or planner for additional information about when to start your diet.

Pre-Op Gastric Sleeve Diet: 3 Weeks before Surgery

In the 3 weeks before surgery, you will usually plan your foods to:

- Reduce Calories -- especially carbs. Carbohydrates are a significant contributor of carbs to many American diets. Processed sugars, such as those in candy and soft drinks, should be removed. Other sources of carbs, such as pasta and breads, aren't bad in and of themselves; however restricting their consumption may have a beneficial impact on your weight.

- Maximize Protein ingestion. Eat 60 or more grams of protein every day. Great sources of protein include chicken, lean ground beef, eggs, as well as poultry.

- Concentrate on healthy fats. It is a fantasy that all fats are bad for you. Some are, some are not. Healthy fats can be found in foods such as fish, nuts, and olives. Other fats, such as those found in oils or butter, should be curtailed. Tran's fats should be avoided entirely.

- Do not dehydrate. Drink loads of water from the weeks before your process. Reduce or prevent soft drinks and alcoholic drinks.

Many programs advocate eating 800 to 1,200 calories per Day And sticking with these tips until a couple of days ahead of your gastric sleeve surgery process. Please consult your program coordinator or dietician for additional information.

Pre-Op Gastric Sleeve Diet: 2-3 Days before Surgery

A Few days prior to surgery you will need to change to an all-liquid diet. Limit your food consumption to broth, water, gelatins, and low carb sports beverages (no sodas). You will want to cut consumption completely starting at midnight on the day of your surgery -- maybe water. Failure to adhere to these guidelines may jeopardize your eligibility to your gastric sleeve process.

What about My Medicines?

Specific medications must also be discontinued before surgery. Included are:

- Arthritis Medicines

- NSAIDs, Including aspirin and aspirin options, such as Tylenol, Advil, Motrin, and Aleve

• Herbal Nutritional supplements

• Anticoagulant (blood-thinning) drugs

Make Sure You ask your doctor for more details and if you have Concerns about drugs restrictions before surgery.

What Can I Eat After Gastric Sleeve Surgery?

Your post-op diet what you consume in the months and weeks Following your gastric sleeve surgery -- is equally as critical as your pre-op dietplan. You may start with fluids and then slowly reintroduce strong foods.

After your post-op diet Is Vital if you would like to realize the advantages of a bariatric procedure. It is going to also help you avoid possible health issues, such as nausea, vomiting, nausea, vomiting, constipation, and gastrointestinal leaks. Here's a week-by-week diet program detailing exactly what to consume following a gastric sleeve surgery:

Post-Op Gastric Sleeve Diet: 1st Week after Surgery

During your first week following surgery, You'll Be limited To clean liquids. Along with water, you are able to drink clean broth, carbonated drinks, as well as the sugar-free variations of beverage mixes like Kool-Aid and Crystal Light. Forgo carbonated drinks, caffeine, and anything with additional sugar.

Post-Op Gastric Sleeve Diet: 2nd Week Following Surgery

The next week will see the inclusion of fluids that are thicker to your diet. These may include such things as applesauce, cream of wheat, Greek yogurt, protein shakes, and sugar-free ice creams and puddings.

Post-Op Gastric Sleeve Diet: 3rd Week Following Surgery

Soft and pureed foods come. Examples include eggs, Ground meats, legumes, fish, cooked veggies, and tender fruits. Other options include hummus and cottage cheese.

Post-Op Gastric Sleeve Diet: 4th Week Following Surgery

Solid foods are finally backed from the fourth week following surgery. Now, the post-op diet is comparable to a presurgical diet. Certain things stay off limits: fried foods, candies, seeds, nuts, whole dairy products, breads, pastas, and fibrous veggies like broccoli. You're permitted to reintroduce caffeine, but just in tiny amounts.

Through the years, you can add a few of those excluded items over but consistently as little pieces. Your focus should stay on lean protein, complex Carbohydrates, and healthful fats. Avoid processed foods and sugar-added products. Eat slowly, chew thoroughly, and stop eating when you quit feeling hungry.

The Big Gastric Sleeve Diet Guide

Gastric sleeve surgery is quick, the results are remarkable Along with the negative risk is reduced, less than 1% severe complication rate in the first 30 days following surgery (Security and Effectiveness of Newer Bariatric and Metabolic Surgery Process).

You're Liver Ahead of Surgery

Your stomach is situated just to the left of your liver. To Access your gut to many bariatric procedures, your physician will use a liver retractor. This is a system that lifts up the liver and out of the way your surgeon can safely work on the gut with no liver becoming whatsoever.

You've Got Non-Alcoholic Fatty Liver Disease

You probably don't know it, but you've got fatty liver disease. If you do not and you are morbidly obese, you are blessed. Fatty liver disease is in which fat cells collect in and about your liver tissues. This causes the liver to work badly.

Additionally, it increases the size of your liver. A Bigger liver Makes gastric sleeve surgery considerably harder and increases the chance of complications.

I have seen a handful of instances where the surgeon determines The liver is so big that it's impossible for them to perform surgery. The surgery either then becomes an open process (non-laparoscopic) or else they cancel and close until the individual makes the decision to follow their two week pre-op diet.

2 Week Pre-op Diet

Why do you have to Be on such a strict diet prior to gastric sleeve surgery? As you're carrying extra weight, so is the liver. And, like stated previously, a huge liver raises your surgical hazard.

However, your liver may very quickly shrink in size in case a rigorous diet is followed. This makes your surgery safer, you fitter, and prepares one to your diet plan the first couple of weeks following surgery.

Average 2 Week Pre-Op Diet

You should always follow your physician's recommended diet 2. Most 2 week pre-op diets urge:

• Boost your protein intake

• Eat lean meats

Lower your caloric intake

• Prevent Breads, pasta, rice, cereals, etc..

Remove Sugars

• Remove Candy, desserts, juices, juices

The list below is a Normal diet fourteen days before gastric sleeve surgery.

• Breakfast

• Protein Shake -- buy a premium excellent protein shake from GNC or alternative nutritional supplement shop in your region.

• Make sure There's not any sugar in the protein shake.

Lunch

• Vegetables and Lean Beef

Dinner

• Vegetables and Lean Beef

Snacks

• You can have a healthful, low carbohydrate snack involving meals.

• Nuts, Berries, veggies, little salad with vinegar and oil, etc..

Fluids

• Stay hydrated. This can help curb your appetite.

• You can normally drink anything sugar free and low in calories.

Bear in Mind, its Extremely Important to follow your two week pre-op diet. This aids your liver, reduces your chance of complications also makes the surgery faster and easier for the surgeon.

2 Days before Surgery

Some surgeons may recommend you stop the next two days Before surgery.

• Carbonated Drinks

• Caffeine

Most physicians will recommend you stick to some rigorous clear Liquid diet beginning two days before your surgery. Clear fluids include sugar free free Jell-Osugar free popsicles, water and maybe 1 protein shake every day. Again, follow your physician's directions.

After Gastric Sleeve Surgery Diet

You have made it beyond surgery and you are on your way into a healthier life. You might believe that it's clear sailing from here. Regrettably, the tough part is just starting.

Now's not the time to cheat. While both week diet has been Significant reduce your chance of surgical (intraoperative) complication, the week to 4 post-op diet can help stop post-op complications.

The first few weeks following surgery, you may experience frequent irritability and it isn't unusual to second guess your decision to have surgery.

The very intense diet after your sleeve gastrectomy Might Appear Like your physician is being too careful. It's utterly crucial that you follow their directions to the'T.'

Cheating in your post-op diet may lead to diarrhea, Dehydration, constipation, bowel obstruction, or an extremely serious gastrointestinal leak. Should you want more inspiration to follow along with own diet, this guide will help.

Below is a Normal diet following gastric sleeve surgery for Weeks 1 to 4 weeks.

Period 1 -- Clear Liquids Only

In week you are restricted to clean liquids only. This seems hard. And it's tough. But most patients have very little need to consume. The hunger hormone ghrelin is all but non-existent following surgery.

The Region of the stomach that produces the Vast Majority of ghrelin is removed during surgery.

Make certain all items listed below are sugar free.

• Water

• Broth

• Jell-O

- Decaf tea

- Decaf Java

- Sugar free Popsicles

- Sugar free beverages which aren't carbonated

You need to avoid:

- Carbonated Drinks

- Really Sweet drinks

- Sugar

- Caffeine

Week 2 -- Complete Liquid Diet with Protein

During week you May begin to feel some desire pains. Continue to follow your physician's recommended diet. Your diet may include all things per week 1 and:

- Protein Powder blended with a sugar free non-carbonated clear liquid.

- Sugar free pudding.

- Soup with soft noodles.

- Non fat yogurt.

- Carnation Immediate breakfast. Start looking for the sugar free alternative.

- Very thin creamed soups.

- Sugar free sorbet.

- Really watery hot oatmeal. Examine the glucose content.

- Diluted No-sugar juice.

- Sugar free, nonfat ice cream

- Thinned applesauce. Assess sugar content.

Week 3 -- Powerful Pureed Foods

Week three following gastric sleeve surgery is demanding. However, the Fantastic news is you may begin incorporating some actual food in your dietplan, albeit pureed.

You still have to take care to limit fats and sugars. The Targets for week 3 comprise:

- Get your 60 grams of protein Every Day

- Eat Gradually

• Introduce Fresh foods one by one.

Food may taste differently and will probably be tolerated differently than they were before surgery. You could realize that milk is more difficult to digest. It is strongly suggested that you introduce new foods gradually.

Give your body a while to respond to every new food. By doing this you're going to have the ability to recognize foods which are causing gas, stomach upset, or diarrhea.

The foods listed below are usually suitable for week Three following surgery.

• 1 protein Shake daily. Now you can combine them together with strawberry or yogurt milk.

• Almond Milk or coconut milk makes a fantastic protein shake.

• Hummus

• Cottage cheese (low fat)

• Soft Cereals -- Allow your own cereal sit at the non-fat milk till it is soft.

• Soft Vegetables -- boil or steam them till they're tender.

• Soft Cheeses -- restrict them, they are generally high in fat.

• Earth Chicken or steak. Insert some steak or chicken stock to maintain the meat tender.

• Soups

• Scrambled Eggs -- these really are a excellent source of nourishment.

• Soft (steamed) fish. Don't forget to think well.

• Canned Salmon and tuna (it's possible to add low fat mayo). Good source of nourishment.

• Mashed fruit. Bananas, avocados, and canned fruit (see sugar content).

You should avoid these foods:

• While Smoothies are fine, restrict their sugar content.

• Sugar

• Starchy Foods like rice, pasta, bread and rice.

• Fibrous Vegetables like broccoli, celery, asparagus, leafy greens.

Week 4 -- Introducing Foods!

You have followed your diet to week. Now it is time to Begin introducing actual foods.

Your stomach and sleeve remain sensitive, so go slow and don't forget to chew each bite completely. You are done with pureed foods, but you need to continue to search for milder versions of food in this week.

- Continue your everyday protein shakes

- Introduce Chicken and steak very gradually. Make sure you feel thoroughly.

- Any kind of fish.

- Fruits

- Vegetables (it is still suggested that you cook them to soften them a bit).

- Sweet Potatoes

- Mashed and baked potatoes.

- Cereal

- Caffeine can be released. It is strongly suggested that you restrict this.

You should avoid the following foods per week:

- Sodas
- Fried foods
- Fibrous Veggies (i.e. celery and asparagus)
- Sugary Beverages
- Chocolate
- Dessert
- Pastas Along with other high carbohydrate, low nutrient foods (pizza).
- Entire milk and other whole milk dairy foods.
- Nuts

Week 4 Healthy Snacks

While It's Suggested that you only eat 3 small meals every day Afternoon and hydrate in-between foods, you might require a tiny healthier snack. If your surgeon accomplishes this, the things below make healthful snacks.

- Hummus With rice crackers or softened (boiled and cooled) baby carrots.

- Hard Boiled egg.

- Quarter Cup of oatmeal.

- Quarter of a baked sweet potato (or microwaved)

- Banana

- Strawberries or fruit.

Week 5 And Beyond

Continue to present Foods one by one to observe how well they're tolerated. Look out for constipation, vomiting, diarrhea, and upset stomach.

• Eat three Small meals daily.

• Hydrate Through the day.

• Cease drinking fluids 30 minutes prior to each meal.

• Prevent snacking. If you do, then select a nutrient-dense food (fruit, vegetable, nuts).

• Take your recommended daily vitamins.

• Make sure you receive 60 grams of protein.

• Supplement daily using a protein shakes.

• Contain Exercise into your everyday routine. Make it a practice.

• Prevent sodas.

• Prepare For poor days. How are you going to cope when you're in a tough situation?

• Locate a Liability partner. Proceed to a service group and make friends which you may call.

6 Tips -- Healthy Eating Following Gastric Sleeve Surgery

1. Pick foods that are nutrient dense. Bread isn't nutrient dense. An banana, apple, fish, etc. . Nutrient dense foods.

2. Don't drink your calories. It will not fill up you and many caloric beverages are full of sugar.

3. Anticipate a Psychological roller-coaster. Do not let food be your relaxation. Produce a Program.

4. Chew your Food completely and take your time eating.

5. Plan what you'll eat if you are going out. Request half of the percentage size. You might find a discount and you will not be tempted to overeat.

6. Make Water your new companion. Drink it frequently through the day. Purchase a reusable 64 ounce jar which it is possible to carry to work together with you. Be sure to complete the whole bottle every day. But remember to not drink with meals (this can help stop stretching your pouch).

Diet Before and After a Gastric Sleeve

Embarking on a journey toward weight loss with gastric Sleeve surgery could be stressful and exciting. Though this process is intended to help patients eliminate weight, it is up to the person to make good dietary decisions, increase physical activity, and shed the weight. Food consumption in the weeks and days prior to and after the surgery ought to be limited and extremely nutritious. Your health care provider will supply more detailed advice once the time comes; however, here is a summary of your diet prior to and following a gastric sleeve.

Two to Three Weeks before Surgery

Begin creating healthful eating habits before entering surgery. Shedding weight before this process lowers the possibility of complications also makes it much easier for the physician to do the surgery. Eating healthful foods ahead also boosts the immune system and accelerates healing time. Plan to modify your diet at least three months ahead of the procedure to permit the time to adjust to the new regimen. Follow the following tips:

- Make healthy food choices as frequently as possible

- Fresh foods and water

- Eat protein

- Eat at least 60 grams of protein every day

- Eat small parts

- Take small bites

- Chew each bite thoroughly

- Eat slowly

- Restrict eating to no longer than three small meals and 2 little snacks daily

- Limit high-fat foods

- Prevent fibrous foods, such as celery, broccoli and asparagus

- Prevent starchy foods, such as pasta, rice and bread

- Avoid greasy or spicy foods

- Prevent sugar

- Avoid entire milk products

- Take a multivitamin

- Drink lots of low-calorie fluids

- Avoid sodas and carbonated beverages

- Restrict caffeine

1 Week before Surgery

In the week before surgery, your diet will change further. In the 1 week mark, you might have to stop taking or switch drugs. Speak with your doctor about the drugs you take to discover if any alterations are essential. Two days before surgery, patients change into a clear liquid diet to begin clearing out the digestive system. At midnight before surgery, patients will need to fully stop drinking or eating anything.

Post-Op Diet Stage One

After surgery, you are going to begin with a clear liquid diet. This can continue from one to seven days depending upon your physician's recommendation. Avoid having a straw or drinking out of a bottle as this may lead to gas bubbles. Always sip fluids gradually, do not worry, and stop if you are feeling complete. You need to eat at least 48 oz of fluids; 64 oz is more preferable. Keep an eye on your fluid consumption and attempt to drink little amounts during the day. Your goal in this period is to remain hydrated and give your stomach time to cure. Approved fluids include:

- Water
- Ice
- Clear beef, vegetable or chicken broth
- Sugar-free beverage blends
- Sugar-free Jell-O
- Flavored water
- Sugar-free popsicles
- Caffeine-free, unsweetened tea
- Thin or diluted juices, such as apple, white and cranberry grape

During this period, you may also start taking nutritional supplements or Vitamins as recommended by your health care provider.

Post-Op Diet Stage 2

Stage two adds heavier beverages and smooth foods into the point 1 diet. The health care provider will decide when patients are prepared to proceed from stage one to stage two. Whatever you at this stage ought to be smooth and soft; the consistency ought to be thin enough to be strained through a sock, but continue to avoid having a straw. Sip slowly and constantly stop the moment you feel complete. Stage 2 includes:

- Protein shakes

- Cream of Wheat

- Smooth cream soup

- Sugar-free Carnation instant breakfast

- Applesauce

- Greek yogurt

- Sugar-free sherbet

- Sugar-free juice, such as vegetable juice and pulp-free orange juice

- Skim or lactose-free milk products

Post-Op Diet Stage Three

With phase three, patients start trying soft foods. Insert new Foods gradually and one at a time to ensure that you are able to handle them. Start by pureeing among the following with broth, water, juice or milk:

- Cooked vegetables

- Beans

- Fish

• Eggs

• Lean ground meats

• Soft fruits following correcting to pureed foods, patients may gradually try soft foods such as fruits, soft fruits, and lean ground meats.

Post-Op Diet Stage Four

In phase four, patients may start slowly testing strong foods and transitioning to a new long-term dietplan, which should follow the exact same wholesome guidelines adopted before surgery. Try one new food at a time to find out whether you can manage it. At every meal, goal to eating at least four ounces of strong foods, but more than eight oz. You need to consume three or more ounces of protein at every meal. Construct up to incorporate all kinds of textures, so remembering to chew your food well before consuming. Most patients are consuming solid foods about a few weeks following surgery.

General Diet Strategies

During the surgery and recovery process, you will find several General guidelines that it is important to remember:

- Introduce a new food at some time
- Chew all food completely
- Eat protein
- Make healthy food options
- Eat three small meals daily
- Drink lots of fluids
- Maintain a food diary
- Eat slowly, a meal should have 20-30 minutes
- Prevent drinking for 30 minutes after a meal

- Stop eating instantly if you are feeling complete

- Quantify foods and fluids

- Use small utensils and plates

- Prevent alcohol

- require vitamins and nutritional supplements as recommended by your Physician

Gastric sleeve surgery can be a Fantastic instrument to assist patients loses weight. Your diet will vary dramatically from the days and weeks surrounding the surgery, however carefully following your physician's directions, learning how to make nutritious food decisions, and remaining committed can produce the weight loss journey a success.

WAY OF EATING

HOW WILL I EAT BEFORE & AFTER BARIATRIC SURGERY?

Surgery Prep

You know there'll be adjustments to how eat following bariatric Surgery, but you might not understand that we request our individual to go to a particular diet leading up to surgery too. This is largely because we want you to eliminate weight which can shrink your liver. You most likely don't even consider your liver when you think about bariatric surgery; however, the liver may play a major part. Your gut is situated near a liver, so in order to perform routine surgery; we will need to precede the liver from the way through the process. Your liver is probably larger than you believe, so the most effective way for us to maneuver your liver from this way would be to get it smaller than it currently is. A huge liver increases your chance of medical complications, and that is the reason why we request you to adhere to a diet which will shrink your liver.

The diet you follow prior to surgery Will Probably be one which prioritizes elevated levels of lean protein, also reduced levels of carbohydrates. A Couple of days before surgery we will ask you to change to a all-liquid diet. That is for your own security and success throughout your bariatric process.

Eating shortly after surgery

Right after surgery you're going to be on a liquid diet. This isn't especially due to weight reduction, but as your insides require a opportunity to heal from surgery. Whether you've got a gastric sleeve or gastric bypass, your gut will have to recuperate from the cutting and stapling we have done. In spite of the entire lap band that entails no cutting of their gut, there's a essential modification and recovery period. The first phase of your post-surgery diet will probably be fluids like tea, water, jello and sugar-free popsicles. Even though it seems like it can be quite tough to remain on fluids only, many individuals discover they feel hardly any appetite throughout the retrieval duration of the procedure.

After the initial retrieval, you will Have the Ability to add beverages Like protein powder blended with water, applesauce thinned out, or fruit juice with no added sugar. The next thing will let you expand into thicker fluids such as protein shakes, soup with tender noodles or fat free yoghurt.

Several weeks following surgery

By this stage your body is going to be recovery from surgery and Most patients are ready to begin adding in more solid, however foods. We advise that you attempt foods one at a time, to give your body an opportunity to adjust. This may also aid you in finding out whether a few foods function for you, and perhaps others are more difficult for you to digest. Some foods that our patients normally try after a few weeks include: low fat cottage cheese, protein shakes, soups, cereal which sits in milk till it is tender, canned tuna fish with reduced fat mayo, and mashed bananas.

Though vegetables are exceptional in general, we'll inquire one to steer clear of fibrous veggies until approximately a month following surgery. Vegetables with a great deal of fiber are more difficult to digest, and also we need your body to really have a simple time as you heal. You will also be requested to avoid starchy food such as pasta or bread, and sugarfree.

Greater than 1 month after surgery

Now you'll be adding an Increasing Number of foods back into Your eating regimen. We'll work with you to make decent food choices, and find out foods that work nicely for your lifestyle. Many individuals find getting sufficient protein is a struggle, so you will want to consider simple proteins such as shredded chicken breast, beans, and canned fish. One other important element is to find snacks that you enjoy, and are easy to catch and take with you. Whenever you've got a day that is packed, it could be tempting to stop and get snacks in a convenience shop, or consume a donut on the job. Rather, make healthy snacks along with you enjoy cakes, string cheese, or person packs of hummus with carrot sticks.

Chapter 3 Dietary Strategies after Bariatric Surgery

It Is Essential to follow the recommended dietary Guidelines after undergoing bariatric surgery. These tips were carefully made by your wellbeing care providers, with the objective of restricting the number of calories you eat, while still providing balanced foods which help prevent nutrient deficiencies and conserve muscle tissue.

General Guidelines

• Eat balanced foods with little parts.

• Adhere to a Diet low in carbs, carbs and sweets.

• Maintain a Daily listing of your food portions along with your protein and calorie consumption.

• Eat slowly and chew little bites of food completely.

• Prevent Bread, pasta, raw vegetables and fresh fruits, in addition to legumes which aren't readily chewed, like steak and pork. Ground meats are often better tolerated.

• Don't Utilize straws, drink carbonated drinks or chew ice hockey. They could introduce air in your pouch and lead to distress.

• Prevent Sugar, sugar-containing foods and drinks, focused sweets and fruit juices.

• For the First two weeks after surgery, your calorie intake must be between 300 and 600 calories each day, with a concentration on thicker and thin liquids.

• Daily Caloric intake shouldn't exceed 1,000 calories.

Fluids

• Drink Additional water and low carb or calorie-free fluids between meals to prevent dehydration. All fluids should be caffeine-free.

• Sip about 1 cup of fluid between every little meal, six to eight times every day.

• We recommend drinking at least 2 liters (64 oz or 2 cups) of fluids each day. You will gradually have the ability to meet this goal.

• We strongly warn against drinking any alcoholic drinks. After surgery, alcohol is absorbed into your system far faster than previously, making its stimulant and mood-altering consequences more challenging to control and predict.

Protein

Encourages muscle tissue by eating foods full of protein. High-protein foods include legumes, fish, poultry, seafood, tuna, poultry, soy milk, tofu, cottage cheese, cheese and other dairy products. Your target needs to be a minimum of 65 to 75 grams of protein every day. Do not be concerned if you can not accomplish this target in the first couple of months following surgery.

Nutritional supplements

You have to take the following supplements on a daily basis to Avoid nutrient deficiencies. Please keep in mind that all pills have to be crushed or cut into six to eight little pieces. You're unable to consume whole pills in addition to before surgery, and it can be problematic for your pills to maneuver through your brand new physique.

Multivitamins

Have a high-potency daily chewable multivitamin and vitamin Supplement which includes a minimum of 18 milligrams of iron, 400 mcg of folic acid, selenium, magnesium and copper. Brands which contain this formulation include Trader Joe's and Centrum Adult chewable multivitamins. Take two pills daily for three or more weeks following your surgery, then 1 pill daily for lifetime.

Calcium Supplement

Require 1,200 to 2,000 milligrams of calcium every day to stop calcium deficiency and bone disease. To increase absorption, then choose the calcium in two to three divided doses during the day - for instance, a 500 to 600 mg nutritional supplement taken three times every day. Calcium citrate is your preferred type of calcium.

Vitamin D Supplement

Have a total of 800 to 1,000 International Units (IUs) of all Vitamin D every day. This entire sum should be taken in divided doses of 400 to 500 IUs two times per day. Vitamin D ought to be taken together with your calcium supplement. If you would like, you may take a mix calcium-vitamin D supplement to prevent taking a number of tablets, provided that it includes the appropriate dosages.

Vitamin B12 Supplement

Require 500 mcg of vitamin B daily. It can be obtained as a Tablet, or in sublingual forms placed beneath the tongue.

Other Nutritional Supplements

Some individuals need extra folic acid or iron Supplements, especially women that are still menstruating. Your dietitian will talk about this with you personally.

Diet Progression after Bariatric Surgery

Immediately after surgery, you may start with a transparent liquid diet. You may slowly begin adding thicker fluids into your diet after you're discharged from the hospital.

Fourteen days after surgery, You Might progress to mix and puréed foods. You can use non-toxic (greater than 20 grams protein), low-calorie (less than 200 calories) liquid nutritional supplements powders or drinks to fulfill your protein needs in this time.

It's important to know that after surgery, your gut Size is quite small - less than 1/4 cup, or on the size of an egg. The opening which allows food to pass from your gut is also quite narrow. Because of this, it's crucial to take two to three sips or snacks at a time of almost any fresh food and wait 10 minutes prior to taking more. This can allow you to learn your limitations and endurance. Liquids will drain faster from your gut compared to soft solids.

Should you overeat or consume too fast, You Might experience nausea or pain. You should avoid rich, creamy fluids like gravies, sauces and ice creams.

Diet at the Hospital

You will receive clear fluids such as juices, Jell-O and Broth as your meal after surgery. Juice and Jell-O are full of sugar content, but your parts will be quite little at this point. Gradually increase the amount you drink at every meal because you are able to tolerate it.

Diet for Your First 2 Weeks Post-Surgery

You Will start adding thicker fluids which are high in Protein and low in sugar and fat. (For examples, see the list under) You may use non-toxic, low-fat liquid nutritional supplement powders or drinks to satisfy your protein needs in this time.

The Objective is to eat modest parts that will drain readily From your spade. Begin with 1 tbsp portion sizes and grow to two tbsp as tolerated. Begin drinking 1/4 cup of liquid at one time and increase into some 1/2 cup tolerated. Your daily caloric intake shouldn't exceed 400 calories.

It's also extremely important to stay hydrated. Drink 1 to 1.5 gallons of water or alternative non-caloric fluids every day.

Recommended heavier fluids:

- Nonfat or 1 percent milk, If You're Able to tolerate milk
- Lactose-free Or soy-based low-fat beverages
- Sugar-free pudding
- Sugar-free, nonfat yogurt
- Low-fat Cottage cheese
- Blended Broth-based soup or alternative low-carb soups

• Enriched hot cereals that are low in fiber, such as cream of rice or cream of wheat. Make them with additional liquid to make a soup-like consistency. Don't eat oatmeal.

• Optional High-protein, low-fat liquid nutritional supplement drinks (beverages containing less than 200 calories and over 20 grams of protein in an 8- to 11-ounce serving).

To increase your protein consumption, add two tablespoons non-fat Dry milk powder, egg substitute or powered egg, or alternative protein powder to every 1/2 cup of nonfat or low-fat milk. You could even add them to soups, hot cereal and other liquids that are thick.

Don't forget to drink 1 cup of water along with alternative non-caloric fluids between meals. Just take a multivitamin supplement daily.

Diet for Weeks 2 to Four Post-Surgery

Begin incorporating very tiny parts of puréed and tender foods as tolerated. Take quite little bites and chew everything really well. Don't take more than two snacks every 20 minutes when adding a fresh food.

Recommended puréed and tender foods:

- Applesauce
- Yogurt
- Cottage cheese
- Well-cooked, puréed vegetables
- Hot Cereals
- Mashed potatoes
- Noodles
- Scrambled Egg whites or egg replacement
- Canned fruits

- Canned tuna fish
- Lean fish
- Tofu
- Lean Ground poultry or meats

Steer clear of all meats and bread which aren't easily chewed.

Recommended dinner Plan for Weeks 2 to Eight until 2 Months Post-Surgery

Currently, your caloric consumption Will Most Likely is no longer Than 500 calories per day, split into six to eight small meals. Recommended part sizes are 1/4 cup for solids and 1/2 cup for fluids.

Sample Menu

This sample menu comprises different foods which are safe for one to consume. You may correct the menu to satisfy your preferences and endurance.

Breakfast

1/4 cup hot cereal made with non-fat milk

Mid-Morning

1/2 cup nonfat milk

Late Morning

Two scrambled egg whites

Lunch

1/2 cup low-fat chicken noodle soup

Mid-Afternoon

1/4 cup low-fat cottage cheese

Late Afternoon

1/4 cup sugar free, nonfat yogurt

Dinner

2 oz lean ground meat

1/4 cup puréed or well-cooked vegetables

Bedtime Snack

1/4 cup caffeinated milk

* Add 1 tbsp non-fat dry milk powder to every 1/4 cup Nonfat milk for extra protein.

Don't forget to drink 1 cup of water along with alternative non-caloric fluids between meals. It's crucial to have a multivitamin and mineral supplement daily, and additional iron if needed, and calcium and vitamin D supplements just two to 3 times every day.

Recommended Diet Plan for 2 to Six Days Post-Surgery

Eat 900 to 1,000 calories and at least 65 to 75 grams of Protein every day. For balanced nutrient consumption, your daily portions should comprise:

- 3 Servings dairy and milk products (nonfat and low carb)

- 3 Portions meat or meat alternative (low-carb and lean)

- 3 Servings starch (restrict rice and bread)

- 1 serving Berry (prevent dried fruits and veggies along with skin)

- Two Portions vegetable (well-cooked only)

Recommended part sizes are 1/4 cup for solids and 1/2 cup for fluids.

Quit taking low-fat liquid nutritional supplement beverages or Powders if at all possible. We recommend meeting your daily protein requirements with food.

Sample Menu

This sample menu comprises different foods which are safe for one to consume. You may correct the menu to satisfy your preferences and endurance.

Breakfast

1 egg or 1/4 cup egg substitute

1/2 cup hot cereal

Mid-Morning

1/2 cup nonfat milk

Late Morning

1/2 cup sliced melon

Lunch

1/2 cup low-fat chicken noodle soup

2 Saltine crackers

Mid-Afternoon

1/4 cup low-fat cottage cheese

1/4 cup canned fruit packed in juice or water

Late Afternoon

1/2 cup sugar free, nonfat yogurt

Dinner

2 ounces lean beef or fish

1/4 cup mashed potatoes

1/4 cup pureed or well-cooked vegetables

Bedtime Snack

1/2 cup nonfat milk

The sample menu provides eight small meals every day. You will want to consume less or more often, but make sure you consume at least six times every day.

Don't forget to drink 1 cup of water or alternative non-caloric fluid between meals. It's crucial to have a multivitamin and mineral supplement every day, and additional iron if needed. Additionally, you should take calcium and vitamin D supplements 2 to three times every day.

Recommended Diet Plan for Six Months Post-Surgery and Beyond

- Continue consuming 900 to 1,000 calories daily

- Reduce To 3 meals and just a couple of snacks daily

- Discontinue Taking low-fat liquid nutritional supplement beverages

- Boost the assortment of low carb, low-sugar and low-fat foods, as tolerated

- Prevent raw Vegetables, fresh fruits with skins, dried fruits, breads, popcorn, nuts and vegetables just if badly tolerated

Long-term Dietary Guidelines

Over time, you'll Be able to increase the amount and Consistency of foods in your dietplan. Some foods might continue to be poorly tolerated, such as red poultry, meats, breads, as well as high-fiber vegetables and fruits. Concentrate on low-carb, low-sugar and low-fat foods and keep to count on your calories daily. Attempt to satisfy your serving aims for many food groups according to the 900 to 1,000 calories diet program described previously.

To remain well hydrated, drink at least 2 liters of water Non-caloric fluids unless that is contraindicated because of a health condition.

Confusions

When You opt to have bariatric surgery, you are taking a Huge initial step toward improved health and psychological well-being. But bariatric surgery is merely 1 portion of this equation. Together with the real surgery, you are also deciding to reset a few of the customs that led one to gain weight in the first place. That is a sign that you are all set to create a shift.

It is common to get questions regarding a diet and meal program post-bariatric surgery. After all, you are going to be creating your grocery lists and eliminating foods in your pantry which aren't bariatric-friendly.

Query 1: What do I eat before continuing surgery?

In the months and weeks before surgery, your connection with food will begin to modify. You'll start to contemplate the way you eat, once you eat, what you eat -- and most importantly why you consume.

Under the advice of a Temple dietitian and bariatric Surgeon, you will also begin to drop weight. While this transformation takes place, you might start to observe a distinct method of thinking in regards to food. This can help prepare you for the months and weeks following weight-loss surgery, as soon as your eating program will change.

Professional tip: Register for a free introductory conference using the Temple Bariatric Program team. You will find out about bariatric procedures like Roux-en-Y gastric bypass and gastric sleeve, and speak with all members of our bariatric staff to learn everything you can.

Question two: After bariatric surgery, will I be hungry on a Liquid diet?

By design, Roux-en-Y gastric bypass and gastric sleeve aid you feel full with less food. And that is a fantastic thing, because shortly after bariatric surgery, your body needs time to rest and heal.

While you're at the clinic, you'll sip 1-2 oz of clear Fluid each hour. Including meats, gelatin and carbonated drinks. After release and for your first week in your home, you are going to continue to grow your fluid consumption -- and your endurance.

Professional tip: Plan to stock your pantry with the Very Same foods you Sipped at the hospital.

Question 3: Can I drink protein shakes following weight reduction surgery?

You will meet with your regular physician 1 week following your procedure. This is a chance for you to ask questions and discuss how you have been feeling emotionally and physically.

It is about that time That You Might Begin to add heavier Liquids to your diet. Including:

- Low-fat creamed soup

- Light yogurt

- Pudding

- And yes -- Protein shakes!

Professional tip: Prior to your surgery, request your Temple dietitian to get Hints on purchasing the proper components, brands and grab-n-go sizes to have available. Stock your pantry and fridge prior to the day of the process.

Question 4: How long after bariatric surgery could I consume strong foods?

You can add pureed foods in your diet in 3-4 weeks after your bariatric process. Pureeing your foods can allow you to get used to textures back, and will prepare one for eating solid foods in a couple weeks.

Begin with protein-rich foods, like fish, poultry, Turkey, eggs and legumes. Around week, you may add a few veggies and fruits.

Pro tip: Prevent fibrous vegetables, such as broccoli. Should you Puree carrots or sweet potatoes, soften them in the microwave or on the stove top in boiling water?

Question 5: What will be the top soft foods to consume after Preventive surgery?

Soft foods are just another step closer to eating solid foods, and are released about weeks 6-8. These include canned or cooked lean meats, fish, poultry, and certain fruit and vegetables.

Pro suggestion: Speak to other people who've experienced weight-loss surgery to get thoughts about what gentle foods that they want to eat. If you're a vegetarian or vegetarian, look at eating legumes and tofu.

Question 6: What foods should I avoid after bariatric surgery?

You may Begin to eat solid foods around week 9 following your procedure. Included in these are the identical sorts of foods you have been eating. Eat protein first, followed by vegetables and then fruit. Focus on how you're feeling as you are eating -- and eat slowly. When you start to feel full, stop eating.

You will need to avoid starchy, high-fat and high-sugar foods. Additionally, it is a fantastic idea to avoid carbonated drinks, such as soda.

Pro tip: When buying solid foods, store the outside borders of the grocery shop.

Conclusion

Gastric sleeve is a sort of bariatric surgery, also referred to as weight loss surgery. It's sometimes suggested for men and women that are extremely overweight, or who have health problems brought on by obesity. You should only consider gastric sleeve surgery after attempting choices. The very first step is typically to test modifications to your food consumption as well as your everyday exercise and activity. Additionally, there are some medications which could help people eliminate weight. Surgery is usually considered just after these other choices are tried. Slimming down after gastric sleeve surgery can help reduce issues with type two diabetes, diabetes episodes and blood pressure, also will help improve heart health. After the surgery, you are going to begin with liquid foods. During the upcoming few weeks you may change to pureed food, then to food. Your meals will be a lot smaller and you might need to quit drinking with meals because of your little stomach. You'll have to make substantial lifestyle changes following bariatric surgery to eliminate weight and keep it off. By way of instance, you are going to receive nutritional advice from a dietitian about the best way best to modify your eating habits to stay healthy while losing weight. Your foods will be a lot more compact than previously. And you're going to likely take vitamins or supplements for life. You'll also need to, and also be in a position to, raise the amount of physical activity that you do.

CPSIA information can be obtained
at www.ICGtesting.com
Printed in the USA
BVHW012019180121
598054BV00001B/33

9 781801 574327